Original title:
A Ring for Every Heart

Copyright © 2025 Creative Arts Management OÜ
All rights reserved.

Author: Fiona Harrington
ISBN HARDBACK: 978-1-80586-130-0
ISBN PAPERBACK: 978-1-80586-602-2

Bridges Wrought of Care

In the land of mismatched socks,
Where laughter bounces like a fox,
We built a bridge from old guitar,
Singing tunes to strum afar.

With every step, a squeaky sound,
Our dance of quirks, we twirl around,
A bridge of care with boisterous cheer,
In silly socks, we conquer fear.

The Soft Curve of Trust

We sat on swings, so high we'd fly,
With trust so soft, it made us sigh,
Each swing a secret, a gentle shove,
Squealing crazy, we fell in love.

From cereal spills to jumpy pranks,
We wrote our tales, made goofy blank hanks,
With every giggle, our bond would grow,
In curly hair and marshmallow glow.

Circles Imbued with Spirit

In a world of doughnuts, glazed with fun,
We twirled and twirled until we spun,
Each circle danced with sprinkles bright,
Spirits soaring, pure delight.

With frosting fights and sugar highs,
We crafted dreams beneath blue skies,
In every bite, our joy was sealed,
With every circle, laughs revealed.

Love's Endless Spiral

Around and around, we spun all day,
In a spiral of laughter, come what may,
Our hearts entwined in giggles and grins,
Chasing rainbows, where fun begins.

With wobbly chairs and jellybeans,
We painted life in silly scenes,
A spiral twist, a dance, a dart,
In every swirl, you found my heart.

Spheres of Serendipity

In a land of circles, round and bright,
We try to find love, oh what a sight!
Some wear it on fingers, others on toes,
While some just play fetch with a hose!

Chocolate chips lie in rings so sweet,
As hugs make their rounds, a merry treat.
But love's just a jigsaw, pieces amiss,
Chasing after frisbees, oh what bliss!

Mementos of the Heart's Odyssey

Off we go, on a love-filled quest,
Finding odd tokens, what a jest!
A gum wrapper here, a rusty old key,
And why is my sock lost—where can it be?

In a box of memories, we rummage about,
Laughter erupts as we figure it out.
A beer cap, an old toy, a lighthouse in sand,
Our hearts collect treasures, oh isn't life grand?

Creations of Love's Craft

With yarn and some glue, we craft with glee,
A hat for the cat, or maybe for me?
Hearts made of muffins, all lopsided and brown,
But hey, they get giggles, who needs a crown?

We build up our worlds with crafts full of cheer,
Paint splatters everywhere, oh dear, oh dear!
But as we create, let none go to waste,
For laughter in chaos is truly the best taste.

Harmonics of the Heart

Strumming on banjos, we sing out loud,
Offbeat and silly, we draw quite a crowd.
With tambourines shaking, we dance in place,
And trip on our laces, oh what a grace!

Fiddles and laughter collide with delight,
As we spin 'round, hearts soaring in flight.
Every missed note is a song of its own,
Making music together, we never feel alone!

Bonds Celestial and Rich

In a galaxy of gold, they twirl,
With bling that makes the stars swirl.
Even aliens take a peek, oh dear,
Wishing for a sparkly souvenir.

Hitching up at cosmic fairs,
With love rings made from moonlight flares.
They trade their bling for a comet's glow,
While giggling, saying, 'Just for show!'

At every orbit, they take a chance,
In whimsical orbits, they breakdance.
With space debris they craft their charms,
Weaving tales that catch the arms.

So let's toast to bonds that shine,
With laughter wrapped in stardust wine.
In this universe of priceless flair,
Love's a concert you can't help but share.

Heartbeats in Harmony

When two hearts meet in silly beats,
They dance like socks on sticky seats.
With rhythm mismatched, they collide,
In honks and giggles, they confide.

Each heartbeat brings a playful kick,
Fumbling notes like a music trick.
With hearts that sync in clumsy ways,
They laugh through all their awkward days.

The serenade of off-key tunes,
As they swoon 'neath the laughing moons.
Their cadence strikes a funny chord,
In the symphony of love, adored.

So let's embrace the tunes we find,
In every jingle, love is blind.
For heartbeats that might stutter and sway,
Create a rhythm that's here to stay.

Love, Unbound and Infinite

In a world where socks go missing,
And every love is a bit dismissing.
With laundry hearts tossed in the fray,
They whirl like chores, come what may.

Giggles flutter like butterflies,
In a garden where affection lies.
They chase each other like silly fools,
Breaking all the love-struck rules.

With daisy chains and pizza dreams,
They sketch out plans, or so it seems.
But as they trip on endless fun,
Love's a race that's never run.

So here's to laughter, crazy and loud,
To bonds that shimmer beneath the cloud.
For in this dance of quirky fates,
Love grows wild and never waits.

Emblems of Affection

In a land where hugs are currency,
Love's a game of silly urgency.
With badges made of giggle spark,
They march along like a vibrant lark.

Each emoji a badge of their quest,
With silly faces put to the test.
In heart-shaped battles, they collide,
With laughter echoing far and wide.

From ice cream cones to dance-off beats,
They dress their hearts in funky sheets.
With piñatas of joy on the street,
Love's a party, impossible to beat.

So here's to tokens, wild and bright,
In every corner, love ignites.
For emblems shared with wacky cheer,
Are whispers of affection, loud and clear.

Shades of Devotion

In a shop with so many gems,
I lost my mind among the stems.
My budget shrank like my old jeans,
But love was worth those crazy scenes.

With diamonds bright and colors bold,
I tried on rings, like some great gold.
One slipped away, oh what a fright!
It rolled me down a funny flight.

Everlasting Echoes

He whispered sweetly, 'Pick a stone,'
But I tripped over a silly cone.
Rings went flying, oh what a sport,
I laughed so hard, 'Twas quite the court!

"Choose gold or silver, rose or blue,"
I said, "Just don't make me choose you!"
With every spin, my choices grew,
All I need is ice cream, it's true!

The Heart's Emblem

I thought I'd find my perfect match,
But every size felt like a catch.
Some fit my dreams, others my nose,
I pouted, stuck in byes and woes.

Then came a ring that made me grin,
It sparkled bright like the deep sea fin.
With hearts as charms and laughs as gold,
Who knew love could feel so bold!

Enchanted Rings of Fate

I strolled through aisles of glimmering light,
Each one promising a future bright.
But then a cat decided to play,
And knocked the display rings away.

Now diamonds dance like silly fish,
While I just laugh and make a wish.
Through laughter loud and moments sweet,
Love's tangled mess can't be beat!

Anchored by Heartstrings

In a drawer full of odd bits,
Lies a tangled mess of hearts,
Some are silver, and some are quirks,
Each a story, a work of arts.

Grandma says they're quite the catch,
But each is slightly out of date,
With hearts that squeak and make a scratch,
Infused with laughter and some fate.

A cheesy grin and wink of eye,
I ask them for a dance tonight,
Two heart-shaped gems start to pry,
Laughing loud, what a delight!

So here we are, with all our flair,
Adorned with symbols, wild and bold,
Nothing holds more than a shared care,
In this tangled love of gold.

Celestial Ornaments

Stars that twinkle in the sky,
Seem to wink and tease my heart,
Yet down below, a cat will sigh,
As I pretend, we never part.

With fuzzy lights on every tree,
I strung them up for all to see,
The ornaments of love's decree,
Each one a joke, tickles with glee.

A moon that smiles, a comet's spin,
They giggle as I trip and slip,
Around my neck, they start to grin,
A jewelry store, a cosmic trip.

With silly songs and jigs to dance,
A sparkling laugh, we take the chance,
To wear our hearts, all have a glance,
In this wacky starry romance.

Bonds Forged in Warmth

A socket here, a plug that fits,
My toaster and I, quite the pair,
We churn out laughs and breakfast bits,
In our kitchen, love fills the air.

With mismatched socks and a warm smile,
Every heart in the house was knit,
In cozy corners, life's a trial,
But each of us just won't quit.

A pen to ink our secret charms,
We joke and poke at every turn,
The softest hug, the warmest arms,
In this dance, we all will learn.

So gather 'round the warmth tonight,
With laughter spilling from the stove,
So bond with me, let dreams take flight,
In this silly side of love.

Oaths Etched in Light

Under flickering bulbs we stand,
Swapping secrets 'neath the glow,
With hearts like summer, hand in hand,
Each chuckle sets the night aglow.

Promises made with a twist of fate,
As clumsily we spin our yarn,
A wobbly dance we celebrate,
In this circus, we disarm.

With silly hats and neon lights,
We vow to cherish, love, and play,
With each cringe-worthy dance that bites,
Our laughter will forever stay.

So raise a glass to hearts alight,
With every hiccup, every spark,
We pen these vows into the night,
In this funny love, we leave our mark.

Jewels of Affection

In a box full of gems, we dive,
Each one a story, still alive.
Some sparkle bright, while others pout,
But all together, they dance about.

A diamond's sharp wit, it might jest,
While rubies boast, they are the best.
Emeralds giggle in shades of green,
As sapphires wink, quite keen and mean.

The pearls just roll with laughter grand,
They say, 'We're classy, can't you stand?'
But in this chaos, love's the glue,
A handful of joy, just for you!

So wear them proud like silly crowns,
In this circus of affection, no frowns.
For every heart that's in the game,
Finds humor here, and love's the name!

Circular Promises

In circles spun with laughter wide,
Where promises swirl and slip, they slide.
Round and round, we twirl and twist,
With each new joke, none can resist.

Like a hula hoop around a waist,
These vows we make, they're filled with taste.
One goes here, and one goes there,
But in the end, we're quite the pair.

A round of applause, the audience roars,
As we dance on stage, with rings galore.
Each twinkle a wink, each blink a dance,
In this endless loop, we take our chance.

Together we spin, and never pause,
In this zany life, we're the applause.
So join the fun, let laughter start,
In every twist lies a joyful heart!

Bands of Love Unfurled

With bands around the fingers tight,
We jest and play from day to night.
Each twist and turn a giggle released,\nIt's tough to keep this joy decreased.

A rubber band with silly tricks,
Bouncing around like playful flicks.
A gold one's shy, it tugs and pulls,
While silver sparkles, it always rules.

Tangled up in a comedy show,
These bands of love only grow and grow.
Some give a stretch, while others snap,
But love's the joke that fills the gap.

So slide your finger on with glee,
In this laugh fest, we're wild and free.
Every twist, a knot of fun,
In the end, we're all just one!

The Embrace of Eternity

In circles wide, we embrace the laughs,
Like donuts shared among good chaffs.
Each giggle wraps us, snug and tight,
In this jestful moment, all feels right.

A hug that curves like a roller's ride,
We spin through jokes, always side by side.
Tickles transmitted, laughter's spark,
In the amusement park, we leave our mark.

Through twists of fate, we hear the clang,
Of funny rings in a joyful sang.
Each chime a reminder, "Don't you fret,"
In this embrace, we're eternally set.

So raise a toast to this merry fest,
In circles of joy, we are the best.
For life's a jest, so let's be bold,
In each embrace, a story told!

Cycles of Love's Embrace

Round and round, we spin each day,
Life's a game, we laugh and play.
In circles tight, our hearts entwine,
Like donut shops, we crave the line.

Silly squabbles, they come and go,
Chasing squirrels, we steal the show.
A wink, a smile, a playful poke,
Love's a circus, and we're the joke.

In the loopy dance, we trip and fall,
Bouncing back, we hear the call.
With each embrace, we twirl and glide,
In our tangled mess, we choose to ride.

So grab your mate and join the fun,
In this wild game, we've already won.
Every swirl and giggle, a brand-new start,
Together forever, you'll steal my heart.

Unbroken Circles

In circles wide, we gather round,
Bad dad jokes, the best resound.
With every laugh, a bond we make,
In our funny dance, no hearts will break.

Like tangled yarn, our stories twist,
With puns so bad, they can't be missed.
Round the table, we share our lives,
Frosting fights, oh how it thrives!

Through ups and downs, we keep it real,
A love so strong, you'd think it's steel.
In our unbroken loops, we spin,
Forever laughing, let the fun begin!

So here's to us, the goofy lot,
In this grand circle, we've got the spot.
With winks and grins, we stand apart,
Together forever, smiling hearts.

The Dance of Infinite Circles

In our dance, we whirl and twirl,
Spinning 'round, just like a girl.
With every step, our hearts collide,
In this crazy waltz, we laugh and glide.

Tripping over each other's shoes,
With silly moves, there's lots to lose.
But hold my hand, we'll laugh it off,
In this merry jig, we give a scoff.

Like infinite loops, we laugh and cheer,
Every misstep brings us near.
With giggles loud, we shake the floor,
In our comical beat, we crave for more.

So let's spin wildly, and chase the night,
In this bright dance, everything's right.
With every circle, we play our part,
Together forever, two silly hearts.

Adornments of the Soul

With mismatched socks, our style's unique,
Silly hats, oh look at me speak!
In jewelry's charm, we find our way,
Every trinket tells tales we say.

Like beads on strings, we connect each day,
In laughter's light, we find the play.
With every giggle, we wrap our hearts,
In these sparkly bits, love never departs.

Chasing squirrels and sharing fries,
In our silly world, the beauty lies.
So dress me up in joy and fun,
In this goofy life, we've already won!

With crazy colors, we shine so bright,
In this wild dance, our hearts take flight.
So raise a toast, let laughter roll,
Together forever, adorn this soul.

The Ties That Bind

In a world of knots and ties,
Where giggles spark and laughter flies,
We stumble on our silly fates,
With hearts wrapped tight in wrinkled plates.

Two left feet dance in crazy pairs,
With mismatched socks and tangled hairs,
We twirl and spin in bold delight,
As love's odd shapes take off in flight.

A toaster squeaks, it sings a tune,
While spaghetti weaves our own cocoon,
With flour dust and joyful mess,
We bond through chaos, we won't regress.

So here's to ties that make us grin,
With twirls, and leaps, we all dive in,
For hearts can tie in the quirkiest ways,
Unearthing fun in every phase.

Gleaming Hues of Connection

Colors splashed, a canvas bright,
Crafting scenes that spark pure light,
With paintbrush hearts, we blend and swirl,
Twirling over every giggly whirl.

Red for love, a gloppy mess,
Yellow laughs, we must confess,
As blue glimmers in skies above,
We find strange art in every shove.

We splash and blot, oh what a sight,
Creating pals in every byte,
With crayons strong, we sketch the day,
A funny twist leads hearts to play.

So let's mix paints and form our crew,
In gleaming hues, our hearts break through,
For friendships bloom in vibrant tones,
As we connect through silly bones.

Inner Whirls of Affection

In dizzy spins of whirly joy,
Our hearts, they dance—each girl and boy,
With laughter's bottle, we concoct,
An affectionate breeze that won't be blocked.

We toss the confetti of crazy dreams,
With silly schemes and ice cream themes,
As kumquat cats and doggy hats,
We waltz around like humor brats.

As thoughts collide in playful jest,
We twirl and whirl, it's for the best,
With goofy grins, we hold on tight,
In hearts' wild spin, we find the light.

So here's to us, in our merry dance,
In inner whirls, we take a chance,
With every twirl and wink we share,
Affection blooms through funny flair.

Reflections of Togetherness

Mirrors laugh at what we see,
Two left shoes in unity,
With splashes of cream on our noses,
We giggle bright as love composes.

In hall of mirrors, faces change,
As funny quirks feel quite strange,
We see our flaws in every gleam,
Reflections bright, like silly dreams.

Side by side, we make a pact,
To laugh at life and never act,
Holding hands through troubled tides,
As friendship's mirror never hides.

So let's embrace what's just absurd,
With every laugh, each twist of word,
In reflections clear, we find our way,
Together strong, we laugh and play.

Round and Round in Love's Dance

In circles we spin, like two clumsy fools,
Our feet get tangled, breaking all the rules.
Each turn a giggle, each spin a delight,
We trip on our toes, laughing into the night.

Our hearts do a tango, with snickers and sliding,
Chasing each other, a whirlwind of gliding.
With every misstep, we bump and we sway,
In this silly waltz, forever we'll play.

Heartbeats Woven in Silver

Our pulses synchronize, like a zany drum,
Each beat a chuckle, oh here we come!
Crafted in mischief, with laughter in tow,
Woven in joy, our hearts all aglow.

With silver threads pulling, we laugh till we cry,
Chasing our dreams, oh my, oh my!
Every heartbeat echoed, a comical tune,
In this ludicrous symphony, we'll dance to the moon.

Whirling in Our Togetherness

We whirl like dervishes, in a mad little spree,
Each goofy grin shared, just you and me.
With arms wide open, we spin and we twirl,
In a dizzying rush, our joy starts to unfurl.

Our giggles get louder, the room spins around,
In this joyous vortex, true love can be found.
Every stumble is laughter, every slip a shout,
In this beautiful chaos, there's never a doubt.

Endless Halos of Affection

Like hula hoops rolling, our love knows no end,
Spinning and bouncing, always on the mend.
With each little bump, affection takes flight,
Our laughter like halos, oh what a sight!

We chase our own shadows, in circles we race,
Wobbling like jelly, our hearts pick up pace.
Forever entangled in this merry refrain,
With rings of our joy, we dance in the rain.

Heartfelt Encounters

In a bustling park where hearts collide,
A squirrel stole a sandwich, what a wild ride!
Lovebirds cooed, while a dog chased a cat,
And laughter erupted—a comedic spat.

With a wink and a nod, they made a pact,
To share their snacks and keep the fun intact.
Hearts on their sleeves, and crumbs on their face,
In the chaos of love, they found their place.

A Tapestry of Circular Love

Two clowns at a fair, with balloons in tow,
One tripped on a shoe, but love took the show.
With pies and confetti, they danced all around,
Spreading joy like paint, on love's canvas found.

The jester juggled hearts, with skill so profound,
While giggles erupted, their laughter unbound.
In a swirl of chaos, they learned a sweet truth,
Love is a circus, full of silly sleuths.

Love Encapsulated in Time

At the clock shop, he spun tales with glee,
Fixing old watches, as charming as can be.
A tick here, a tock there, time had a flair,
He made sure each heart was handled with care.

With goofy expressions, they'd misplace their keys,
But shared many laughs, like a warm summer breeze.
Time danced in circles, love's rhythm was true,
In every tick-tock, a surprising view.

A Circle of Souls

In a coffee shop, two friends shared a seat,
Spilling their drinks was a comical feat.
With caffeine-fueled giggles, they plotted their scheme,
To toast to their friendship, and live out a dream.

With doughnuts in hand, they bargained for fun,
"Whoever eats last, buys coffee for one!"
Their banter was catchy, their smiles so bright,
In the circle of souls, they found pure delight.

Vows Illuminated

In a chapel made of cheese,
We promised not to sneeze.
With macaroni as our band,
We dance, hand in hand.

Our vows were a silly show,
With jellybeans in tow.
"I do," I said with glee,
While slipping on a brie.

A cake of frosting piled high,
We laughed 'til we were dry.
In hats shaped like a pie,
Oh my, oh my, oh my!

A garland made of taffy bright,
Brought giggles through the night.
Two hearts, a pair of clowns,
In candy-coated crowns.

Vinyl of Heart's Melody

Our love spins like an old record,
A scratchy tune that's absurd.
With each skip and silly sound,
We dance round and round.

In mismatched socks we twirl,
Like two odd-shaped pearls.
With a beat that never ends,
We laugh with our friends.

Dancing on a wobbly floor,
We just can't take it anymore.
Each twist brings a new surprise,
As laughter fills our eyes.

Oh, the songs we've sung so loud,
To our quirky, funky crowd.
With hearts full of silly dreams,
We float on laughter's streams.

Cycles of Affection Unbroken

We pedal through love's sweet maze,
    In silly, wobbly ways.
  On trikes with bells that ding,
    We giggle and we sing.

  Two hearts racing in the sun,
    With ice cream—what a fun!
  As cones drip on our laps,
    We dodge sticky mishaps.

With spokes that squeak and squeal,
    We circle, sharing a meal.
  In tandem bikes we ride,
    With laughter by our side.

Through muddy puddles we splash,
    With every unexpected crash.
Still, we find our way back home,
    In our silly love, we roam.

Echoes of Togetherness

In a park where laughter springs,
We echo all the silly things.
With shadow puppets on a wall,
We make each other fall.

Our jokes bounce like a ball,
With punchlines that enthrall.
We roll down hills with glee,
Just as crazy as can be.

In picnics under the trees,
We share our light-up cheese.
With ants that steal our snacks,
We plot our little hacks.

The echoes of our silly cheer,
Bring hearts together near.
In every giggle shared at dusk,
Our love's bright, fun-filled husk.

Eternal Whirls of Passion

In a dance of love we twirl,
Spinning like caffeinated squirrels.
With every step, we giggle loud,
Two clowns lost in a loving crowd.

Your heart's a puzzle, a messy part,
Like trying to bake without a chart.
Yet here we are, mismatched with flair,
Each quirk an art, a loving pair.

We share our snacks, one too many fries,
While cake crumbs tumble, oh what a surprise!
Laughter echoes through our days,
In our little world, it's a messy maze.

So let's keep spinning ever so bright,
In this circus of love, a sheer delight!
Together we'll dance till the stars align,
Holding tight as we sip on cheap wine.

The Glow of Union

Two misfits wandering, what a scene,
Like cats and dogs, we form a team.
With flashlights on our heads at night,
We search for snacks, oh what a sight!

Your laugh's a glow, like a firefly's shine,
Warming my heart, oh so divine.
We build our life with silly schemes,
Mismatched socks and wild, wild dreams.

With each toast, we toast to the silly,
Your silly dance just makes me giddy.
In this glow, no need for a chart,
Together we stay, oh what a start!

As the world spins round and round,
We find our joy in the absurd found.
In the chaos, we laugh and cheer,
Creating memories year after year.

Mosaic of Shared Dreams

Our dreams are like a crazy quilt,
Stitched from laughter, love, and guilt.
With mismatched pieces, we create,
A masterpiece, let's celebrate!

You snore, I scheme, what a delightful mess,
Like two jigsaw pieces, we feel blessed.
In the chaos, we find our tune,
Like cats on a roof under a full moon.

With every argument, a patch we sew,
Turning squabbles into a comedy show.
From cereal spills to burnt-out toast,
Leftover love is what we boast!

Together we build our life so grand,
A mosaic of nonsense that we've planned.
And as we laugh, our hearts will gleam,
In this beautiful, silly dream.

Anointed with Devotion

In this love, we're a tad bizarre,
Like two goofy peas in a pickle jar.
Anointed with care, we stumble and trip,
Your heart is my home, my favorite trip!

With you, I've learned how to balloon,
To laugh while we shuffle to the moon.
Oversight flourishes in our sweet blunders,
Turning each mishap into thunderous wonders.

Your wink is a treasure, your quirks are gold,
Together we weather, grow bold amidst old.
Through ice cream fights and pillow debates,
We shape our world with laughter in spates.

So here's to us, the oddball crew,
Dancing through life, with love that's true.
Anointed with luck, we rise to the sky,
As laughter rings out, we'll always fly high!

Glints of Shared Dreams

In a shop of shiny things,
We found two silly bands,
One sparkles like a donut,
The other, a rubber band.

We laughed as we tried them on,
Their sizes were quite absurd,
On our toes and on our ears,
All it took was one small word.

You said yours looked like sunshine,
I claimed mine's a rainbow's friend,
Together we sported mismatches,
Our fashion, a funny trend.

So here's to those shiny wonders,
The treasures that never start,
With every giggle shared together,
We have twinkling glints at heart.

Ties that Illuminate

I bought a string of marbles,
Thought they'd serve as our new ties,
Each a shade of what we love,
Stuck in pockets, a sweet surprise.

You thought they'd make us fancy,
Like royalty, oh so grand,
But we tripped on our ambitions,
And laughed 'til we could barely stand.

We tied them round our fingers,
A loop of silly glee,
With each twist and turn together,
Who knew ties could be so free?

So here's to our bright connections,
A string of joy we share,
In a world so full of laughter,
What's a tie? Just love laid bare.

Hours in a Heartbeat

A watch that runs on jellybeans,
Counts time with every chew,
The hours pass as sweetly,
With every tasty view.

We laughed about the seconds,
If tangy or if sweet,
At every tick we crunched a bite,
A calendar of treats!

Unraveled all our thoughts,
In flavors old and new,
Who needs a fancy timeline,
When time's a smile or two?

So here's to joy in minutes,
With laughter as our guide,
Each hour spent together,
In sweetness, joy, and pride.

For Every Beat, a Jewel

A heart that skips like little rocks,
    For every laugh we share,
A gem that shines with silly quirks,
    Sparkling light in the air.

You said your heart's a silver bell,
    Mine's a candy-coated drum,
    Together we create a tune,
    That's silly, bright, and fun.

We dance in our mismatched shoes,
    As jewels fly left and right,
With every clumsy step we take,
    We shine through all the night.

So here's to every heartbeat,
    That sings our special song,
In laughter, love, and friendship,
    With every beat, we belong.

Circles of Connection

In circles we gather, oh what a sight,
With laughter and love, everything feels right.
Little trinkets abound, so shiny and real,
Do they bring fortune, or just a meal?

Each circle a story, spun round and round,
Like a hula hoop contest, we all tumble down.
A pendant of promise, a bracelet of glee,
Is it jewelry, or did I just pee?

Connections like loops, entwined in our fate,
That one friend who shows up an hour late.
We trade all our treasures, a wild card or two,
"Who needs fancy rings? I've got this glue!"

So let's toast with laughter, let's toast with flair,
To circles of chaos, and rings made of air.
For every giggle's worth more than gold,
In the circus of hearts, our tales are retold.

Tokens of Eternal Promise

With tokens in hand, we jest and we play,
A rubber band promise, it's here to stay!
To treasure a snack, or a moment so sweet,
I bartered my sandwich with you for a seat.

A sticker from school, it's a glorious find,
I'll trade you this token if you don't mind.
Eternal delights, with a laugh and a cheer,
Just make sure your promise isn't an old smear.

Tokens of joy, we toss to the sky,
Some fly like a kite, others just say "bye!"
With each silly gift, we laugh till we snort,
Is that love in the air, or just a shoe court?

Let's juggle our dreams, with a giggle or two,
A friendship like ours is a colorful brew.
So raise a big laugh, for connections so fine,
With tokens of joy, our two hearts entwine.

Jewels Beneath the Surface

Digging for jewels beneath all the grime,
We find shiny trinkets, oh, what a time!
But the funniest finds, they always take shape,
Like a rubber duck dressed in a cape.

A treasure chest filled with old dusty shoes,
Did I find something great, or did I just lose?
With laughter we sift through the odds and the ends,
Finding more cups than actual friends.

Underneath all the laughter and sparkly sheen,
Lie secrets of friendship, or is it just beans?
The real gems we find are the bonds that we weave,
Through moments so silly, can you believe?

So let's keep on digging, we treasure our night,
With gigs and with glimmers, our hearts take flight.
For it's not about riches or diamonds that gleam,
But the goofy adventures we all love to dream.

Whispers in the Band

In a band of misfits, we dance like a fool,
With whispers of secrets, we create our own rule.
"Pass me the chips!" turns to "What's in your hat?"
With each silly joke, we become more than that.

A flash of a wink, a smirk in the dark,
Our laughter resounds like a cheerful lark.
"Hold my hand tight!" I shout with delight,
As we fumble our way through the wild moonlight.

The rhythm of friendship, a melody bright,
Each giggle a note, to make our hearts light.
With whispers and chuckles, we march to the groove,
Is it my song, or did you just move?

So let's forge a tune that's both goofy and grand,
With whispers of laughter, let's take a stand.
In this band of our hearts, we'll never depart,
For the joy of connection starts deep in the heart.

Radiance of Unseen Ties

In a world of bling and flair,
Some folks wear nothing but air!
But when they shine, oh what a sight,
Invisible glam that feels just right.

Friends exchange bands, it's quite the scene,
Like laughter wrapped in gold, so keen.
A chuckle here, a wink or two,
Ties of love that are always true.

Forget the diamonds, just grab a thread,
Laughter's the gem, let joy be spread!
Each silly dance, each goofy grin,
Promises made, let the fun begin!

So next time you think of sparkly ties,
Remember the giggles, oh how time flies.
It's not the glimmer that lights the way,
But the funny moments that choose to stay.

Celestial Bonds and Beacons

Stars twinkle bright, eyes all aglow,
Who needs space rocks when you can show?
A rubber band stretches with a twist,
Proof that joy can't be missed!

Cosmic friendships, quite the exchange,
Their strength and humor, never strange.
Each loop of laughter ties us tight,
In this galaxy, we feel just right.

Comets and kisses, laughter so sweet,
Making memories on every street.
So grab a friend and start to play,
Life's a circus in its own way!

And whether we shimmer or shine,
It's the friendships that truly align.
With beacons of joy, forever spark,
We'll dance through the universe, leaving our mark!

The Language of Circular Gifts

Circles are funny, they could have been squares,
But then we'd be tangled in all of our cares.
Round and round, we go in delight,
Gifting our smiles, oh what a sight!

A hula hoop twist, a merry-go-round,
Every loop we make, more fun to be found.
A circle of pals, oh what a troupe,
Like spaghetti noodles in one big swoop!

Tied up in giggles, each round we take,
A ride on this merry-o-snake.
Each hug we share, a circle we weave,
In this round world, together we believe!

So let's keep circling, hand in hand,
With every chuckle, our hearts expand.
For in this loop, we know it's true,
The fun is eternal, just me and you!

Portraits in Precious Metal

A portrait of friends, shiny and bright,
Capture our moments in pure delight.
Some bling may tarnish, some styles may fade,
But the laughter remains, a priceless cascade!

Polished up jokes, a smattering of glee,
Our memories glow like a gilded decree.
Thick chains of friendship, woven with ease,
Adventures together, always a breeze!

We strut with flair, each laugh echoes loud,
Walking our path, oh, so proud.
Each twist of fate, with a wink, we see,
This comedy stage is just for me!

So hang these portraits, oh what a view,
In this gallery of life, it's just me and you.
For every frame holds a joke that we share,
In the museum of laughter, nothing can compare!

Love's Gemstone Legacy

In a shop of quirky charms,
Where each bauble has its quirks,
I sought a gem to hold my heart,
But left with a cat that lurks.

A diamond claims to shine the best,
But I found a funny rock,
It sparkles with a lopsided jest,
I wear it like my pet parrot's sock.

Colors swirling like a whirlpool,
Every hue is a new delight,
But my friend just asks, "Are you a fool?"
I reply, "Just trying to wear it right!"

With every glance, it brings a cheer,
"No wedding plans, I swear, not quite,
Just a reminder that love is near,
And laughter's better in moonlight!"

Embrace of the Infinite

In the cosmos, love takes flight,
With a twist and a cosmic dance,
Some rings just cause a plight,
Like one that's lost in candy's trance.

Infinity wraps its arms so wide,
A platform for a jumpy heart,
But when pancakes flew, oh what a ride!
Now I'm stuck in breakfast art.

"Why wear these circles made of gold?"
When brownies ask for attention,
A heart-shaped cake? It never gets old,
And yet, it's quite the contention!

But in laughter, a bond that lasts,
As giggles echo through the air,
A sweet embrace that shatters the past,
And life's a comedy, if you dare!

Bound by Celestial Threads

Stars twinkle like mischief in night,
Each one tells a tale of love,
But I'd rather wrap them tight,
In a blanket and laugh like a dove.

Constellations like friends in disguise,
Trying to catch my heart in a net,
But who knew they were such klutz guys?
I've got a heart not ready to fret.

Shooting stars crash with laughter bright,
As I make wishes, sticky and sweet,
I find that love is pure delight,
Especially when wearing mismatched feet!

So here's to threads that tie us close,
With each giggle that fills the space,
In the universe's merry dose,
I'll take love wrapped in a comic embrace!

An Oath in Gold

Promised forever, but what does that mean?
When shiny bands can make you sneeze,
I wore it while cooking, oh what a scene,
Now it's stuck in my dough, if you please!

Golden vows have a twist of fate,
They gleam with a giggle and wink,
But try to peel off that floury plate,
And you'll find it's stuck, don't even blink!

Dancing around with a pot in hand,
Spinning tales that sparkle and spin,
An oath that's funny, all unplanned,
As I juggle love, where do I begin?

So here's to a bond that's never dull,
With laughter woven in every squish,
Love's a circus, a gleeful pull,
And I'm the clown, making my wish!

Woven Threads of Unity

In every market, there's a gem,
A deal that makes you say, "Oh, them!"
But look a bit closer, you will find,
The sparkles hide the tales entwined.

With aunties knitting, eyes all aglow,
Thinking of rings? Just say, "No, no!"
For patterns woven bring double the cheer,
Like two left shoes losing their career.

Tangled emotions, a thread unraveled,
Got lost in the stash? Oh, how we traveled!
Stitches of laughter in a pattern of woes,
A knit or a purl, everybody knows!

So gather around for a chuckle or two,
Embrace the misfits, the colorful crew!
In this circle of craft, we're all intertwined,
With each stitch, a memory delightfully defined.

Bonds Beyond Time

Once on a trip, I lost my shoe,
But what I found? A band of blue!
Not just for fingers, but also my toe,
A fashion faux pas that stole the show!

In cafes, folks sip their coffee strong,
"My ring's too tight," they laugh along.
With fingers crossed, they ask for a bite,
Of pastries layered, a truly sweet sight.

Through ages past, our tales align,
With mismatched socks and skirts that shine.
Bonds beyond time, like cheese and wine,
The quirky friendships taste divine!

So toast to the moments, both silly and grand,
We laugh with our rings, a misfit band.
In this dainty dance, we twirl and spin,
For the bonds we wear are the truest win!

Infinite Journeys in Metal

In a shop of wonders, I spotted a charm,
Promised to keep all my worries calm.
But what did it do? Just dangle and sway,
A hipster's delight, in a curious way!

Metallic spirals that twist and twirl,
One says, "I'm bold!" The other, a pearl.
On trips around town, they trade silly tales,
Of pizza mishaps and old, dusty trails.

A traveler's dream in shiny attire,
Got lost in the details, but never in fire.
With laughter erupting as we stroll through the plaza,
The metal dreams spin in a wild fiesta!

So pack up your quirks and let's hit the ground,
In this garden of randomness, joy can be found.
These journeys for hearts, all twisty and neat,
In laughter, we bond, to our own funky beat!

Cherished Cycles of Emotion

In a world of circles, we laugh and we cry,
"Can I wear two today?" my friend asks with a sigh.
Caught in a loop of our own little schemes,
With rings in our pockets, we chase our own dreams.

The cycle of joy, oh, how it spins 'round,
From pastry shops to our favorite town.
We measure our moments in shiny delights,
Exchanging the secrets on long, starry nights.

With each little slip, we giggle and fawn,
"What fits on my ring will fit on this lawn!"
In misplaced jewels, our hearts find their beat,
Creating a rhythm that's fabulously sweet.

So here's to those circles, both old and new,
Each twist brings a story, and a hearty view.
In cherished embrace of our humorous plight,
We dance through the cycles of day into night!

Emblems of Unbroken Vows

In a shop of shiny trinkets,
Promises shine like bright new pennies,
Some folks try on every piece,
Thinking, 'Will this bring me many Denny's?'

A gold band slips on a pinky,
While another's stuck on a toe,
Is love just a game of dress-up?
Or a circus with a three-ring show?

Each bauble spins a tale or two,
From clumsy knights to queens so bold,
They whisper secrets, all in jest,
About the charms of vows retold.

So gather 'round for laughs and cheers,
For metal won't have the last say,
It's the fun in loving wrongly
That makes our hearts dance and sway.

Love's Gleaming Band

Two shiny circles wrapped in mime,
Certainty sealed with a playful rhyme,
Do they bring joy or just a laugh?
In love's game, we're all a gaffe!

One's size too big, the other too small,
They tumble like clowns at a carnival stall,
Stuck to fingers or even a nose,
Making memories as laughter explodes.

So here we are in a sparkle parade,
With wobbly vows and promises made,
Each ring a portal to giggles galore,
Unlocking laughter unlocked the door.

With every twist and clink they make,
We vow to prank love without a shake,
These bands of humor tell stories bright,
In our circus of love, everything's right!

Chains of Heartfelt Bonds

Links of laughter, shiny and stout,
Every story begins with a bout,
Funny how love sometimes feels like chains,
But giggles are our escape in rains.

Worn on a wrist or around a neck,
Each bond's a clown in a big old trek,
Jokes tethered tight with heart's delight,
Tickling whispers in the warm moonlight.

Some chains are loose, while others cling,
Wrap us in mischief and the joy they bring,
For in every twist, there lies a spark,
A love that's silly, leaving its mark.

So let's celebrate this merry plight,
With giggles over every heartfelt right,
These chains we wear with glee and flair,
Are just the proof we love to share.

Circular Journeys

Round we go on love's weird ride,
With loops and swirls, who needs a guide?
Every turn a giggle fits,
As we trip over our laughing wit.

In circles, we chase our silly fate,
Falling down while trying to skate,
Each rotation brings a new dance,
In the merry chaos of romance.

Paths entwined like pretzel shapes,
Laughter erupts as each heart escapes,
Love's a merry-go with painted smiles,
Spinning us round for miles and miles.

So take my hand, let's swirl and play,
In circles of joy, come what may,
For every loop's a splendid start,
In our fun-filled ride of heart to heart.

The Embrace of Infinity

In a shop filled with trinkets and charms,
I found one that twinkled, it had such sweet harms.
Thought it was a bracelet, but oh what a twist,
It turned out a ring that I simply can't resist.

With glittery sparkles, it caught all my eye,
Trying it on, I gave it a shy try.
Then it slipped off my finger, went rolling away,
Right into the cat's bowl, oh what a display!

The chase was on for my whimsical prize,
The feline ambushed me with its sly little lies.
I nearly fell over, and knocked down a shelf,
Is it really love if I end up by myself?

But there in the chaos, laughter took flight,
A sweet little spark in the midst of the fight.
No better reminder of joy and its quirk,
Than a ring with a cat who prefers it for work!

Wedding of Heart and Soul

Two hearts in a dance, like socks in a wash,
They spin and they tumble, creating a smosh.
"Do you take this?" the question they ask,
While I'm just confused by the shape of this flask!

With vows written on pizza and cake made of cheese,
They pledged their sweet love with giggles and wheeze.
But oh, what a sight when the ring went a-fly,
Right into the punch, goodbye sparkling sky!

Their friends all erupted in synchronized cheers,
While one mate was fishing, swigging down beers.
"Your love's like this drink, always fizzy and bold,
But careful! Don't drown, that's not how it's told!"

Yet still they remained, with hearts brave and true,
Through laughter and mishaps, together they grew.
A wedding of souls, in chaos they thrived,
A funny affair where love truly arrived!

Love's Everlasting Embrace

Two people collided, right in the booth,
Love wrapped them up, just like spoons with some truth.
They shared jokes and giggles, each moment a blast,
But soon at the bar, their drinks flew quite fast!

"Watch out!" cried the waiter, quite amazed by the scene,

As a ring took a leap, it felt like a dream.
It bounced on the table, then straight out the door,
"Hey! Do you need this?" yelled a guy on the floor!

With laughter erupting, they chased it down bold,
In a wild game of tag, as the night turned to gold.
They danced through the streets, chasing love with delight,
In rings, hearts, and one crazy evening so bright!

Then back at the bar, they settled down fast,
The ring now secured, in a toast to the past.
With a laugh and a wink, they sealed the sweet fate,
For what is true love but a twist of good fate?

Serene Orb of Affection

Upon a relaxing, sunshiny day,
Two pals stumbled in to find fun in the fray.
With lemonade sipping, and donuts quite near,
A ring caught their eye, they laughed loud with cheer.

"It's perfect!" one shouted, "let's get it for me!"
While the other just giggled, "That's meant to be free!"
But as quick as a wink, the ring flew up high,
And landed on a squirrel, oh my, oh my!

The furry mischief-maker dashed off with a grin,
While the friends were left laughing, they'd never give in.

"We'll catch that small thief, and reclaim what's ours,
With cake by our side, we'll run through the stars!"

Through park benches, bushes, and epic ring chases,
They turned the whole day into thrilling embraces.
With joy in their hearts, they danced through the sand,
For the best kind of love is the silly, unplanned!

Whispers in the Circle

In the circle we gather, a quirky lot,
With shiny bands that fit quite hot.
Some twinkle, some jiggle, some even squeak,
Each one tells a tale, absurd and unique.

There's the one shaped like a twisty pretzel,
It's perfect for snacking, oh what a vessel!
Then there's the bling that winks just so,
It grins back at me like, 'Hey, let's go!'

In a world where laughter wraps us tight,
Our quirky adornments sparkle bright.
With every gesture, a giggle springs,
Oh, the joy that silly jewelry brings!

So here's to the laughter and the playful gleam,
To rings that are more than they may seem.
Join the circle, let your inner child play,
With every chuckle, chase the gray away!

Echoes of Tenderness

Whispers of love float in the air,
Twinkling bands, a rock-solid pair.
One's got a charm shaped like a fish,
The other's a heart, quite the tasty dish!

We dance around, changing colors and hues,
In this adorable circus with whimsical views.
Each ring a story, a giggly delight,
Promising mishaps under moonlight bright.

With every spin, new laughter ignites,
Our rings become rockets, taking flight.
One bounces off walls like it's found its groove,
The others just giggle, watch its move!

A cat wearing a collar that sparkles and shines,
Sips on the joke, as the rings intertwine.
For in this chaos of echoed spark,
Even the moon chuckles and gives a lark.

Infinite Loops of Devotion

Around and around, like a silly tune,
Our bands of loyalty dance to the moon.
Got a loop that resembles an endless pretzel,
A twist that could spark a whimsical vessel.

Each ring's got a secret, a giggle or two,
Like 'Just married!' or 'I'll take that shoe!'
One jingles with joy, another with flair,
Each ring tells the world, 'We make a great pair!'

In the joyful embrace of this whimsical space,
A few bands have found their rightful place.
The punchline is simple, the humor's divine,
It's a party for fingers, like sip-wine-and-dine!

So wear your quirks like a badge of delight,
Let them shine bold in the soft, starry night.
For love has no rules, just giggles in store,
A band for your laughs, and maybe one more!

Adorned with Heartstrings

With heartstrings adorned, we leap and we spin,
Each ring's a licorice twist — where to begin?
One looks like a donut, glazed and round,
Munchkin giggles echo, happiness found!

There's a band that honks when you shake your hand,
It joins in the laughter, oh, isn't it grand?
With charms that clink like a tap dancing shoe,
What a delightful cacophony we're in too!

As we dance through the folly of shapes and of gold,
Each piece holding stories, and nonsense untold.
The quirky adornments like stars in the night,
Spin tales of merriment, pure delight!

So, let's raise a toast with fingers ablaze,
To friendship and laughter in silly displays.
For in every loop, every twirl, every cheer,
We find a new joy as our hearts draw near!

Encircled by Emotions

In a world where hearts collide,
Everyone wants a love to ride.
But what's the deal with all this fuss?
Are we all just here to discuss?

With diamonds and gold, we strut our stuff,
Yet love can feel just like a bluff.
Who needs a sparkly big ol' rock?
When laughter's the key, let's take stock!

From quirky dates with nacho cheese,
To dancing awkwardly in the breeze.
We're trapped in loops, you see our charm,
In silly antics, we find our calm.

So, let's embrace the ridiculous ride,
With hearts entwined, let's take pride.
In the nonsensical things we can share,
Together we laugh without a care!

Circles of Belonging

We gather in circles, so round and bright,
Searching for joy, from morning till night.
With quirky quips and jests in tow,
We spin our tales, letting laughter flow.

A dance-off with socks, we twirl around,
In absurdity's arms, true love is found.
Who needs a label or a romantic plan?
Just join the circle, be part of the clan!

Imaginary crowns on our silly heads,
Together we sleep in mismatched beds.
With laughter and quirks, our hearts unite,
Circled by joy, everything feels right.

So, grab a friend, take a chance,
In circles of belonging, let's dance.
No rings required when friendship's the key,
The circle of laughter is all we need!

The Promise of Forever

With gummy bears and old inside jokes,
We swear to stick like super glue folks.
Promises made over burnt toast,
In the kitchen where we laugh the most.

Forever feels like a dance on a spree,
Though sometimes it's just a quick (and mad) tea.
In the chaos of life, with moments that spark,
We find forever in the humor, not dark.

Who knew that love could look so absurd?
With quirks and giggles, all left unheard.
We dissect dreams with wild, silly grace,
And make forever a whimsical chase.

So here's to the promise we make each day,
A laugh together, come what may.
Forever's a joke, it's true from the start,
In the jest of our lives, we find the heart!

Threads of Infinite Connection

In the web of life, we weave and play,
Connecting through humor in our own way.
With threads of laughter, we spin the yarn,
Creating bonds that never can harm.

Like spaghetti thrown against the wall,
Some stick, some slide, but we love them all.
In each tangled moment, joy takes flight,
Offering warmth in the cool of the night.

We thread our hearts with jests and smiles,
Journeying together for miles and miles.
With silliness guiding our path each day,
Infinite connection leads us astray.

So take my hand, let's unravel the fun,
In this quirky dance, we have just begun.
With laughter as our thread, we shall never part,
The fabric of friendship threads deep in our heart!

Dia of Shared Moments

In a world where socks must twirl,
Two mismatched pairs, they swirl and whirl.
Coffee stains and crumbs in bed,
Best friends laughing, never dread.

Gnomes in gardens sing their song,
We dance around, it won't be long.
With every quirk and funny fall,
A symphony of joy, we call.

Pasta plates that slide away,
We chase them down, a food ballet.
A wink, a giggle, all the cheer,
In moments shared, we persevere.

Through silly dances and cupcake fights,
Our lives entwined under starlit nights.
With every laugh and goofy grin,
Together always, let's begin!

Radiance of Closeness

You're my sunshine on a rainy day,
Even when socks go astray.
We bicker over what to watch,
But popcorn battles—oh, what a notch!

In jammies soft, we end the night,
Your snoring's truly a funny sight.
With cozy blankets wrapped so tight,
We giggle in the pale moonlight.

Your jokes, they sometimes fall flat,
Yet I adore your quirky chat.
Loud laughter echoes off the walls,
In every stumble, love just calls.

We jaunt through parks and stand by swings,
With silly hats, oh, what joy brings!
Two goofballs sharing punnish fate,
In our shared moments, life's so great!

Love's Infinite Arc

In this dance of fumbles, we thrive,
The way you trip, we come alive.
With every twist and silly spin,
You snicker loud, your goofy grin.

Through muddy puddles, we jump in bright,
Your splashy moves—a true delight!
With arms wide open, hearts so light,
In laughter's glow, we take our flight.

Your secret dance, oh what a sight,
An owl in boots: what pure delight!
Together, we feast on cake and pie,
With joy that makes the dreariest fly.

We craft our tales with every glance,
In awkward moments, we find romance.
With every step, a heartfelt chuckle,
Our love endures, forever buckle!

Luminescent Whispers

Under moonlit skies, our giggles flare,
When you try to dance, I can barely bear.
With whispers soft and tickles too,
The night ignites; it's me and you.

In the kitchen, chaos reigns supreme,
Flour explosions, our cooking dream.
With every mess, a bond so sweet,
In this love, we feel complete.

You say you can't cook, but take a chance,
With burnt toast, oh, the glorious romance!
But in our hearts, the flavors soar,
For laughter's taste is worth much more.

Through every quirk and playful tease,
Together, we conquer all with ease.
In every jest, a loving spark,
Our banter shines; it lights the dark!

Around the Fire of Unity

We gather 'round this fire bright,
Each tale ignites a laughing sight.
With marshmallows stuck to our noses,
We share our dreams, like blooming roses.

The sparks fly up, oh what a show,
We dance like crabs, moving slow.
But in this warmth, we find our cheer,
A circle formed, with friends so dear.

Jokes are tossed like logs of wood,
Some hit the mark, some really should!
But every laugh, a shared delight,
Our hearts are light, our bonds are tight.

So let the fire crackle and hiss,
In this chaos, we find our bliss.
We're all a bit loony, that's no debate,
But this joyful madness we celebrate!

Tidal Waves of Loyalty

When the tides roll in, we wade with grace,
Splashing around, we make silly faces.
With loyalty strong as the ocean's wave,
We paddle together, oh how we behave!

Salt in our hair and sand on our feet,
We do the crab walk, oh what a feat!
Though waves may tumble, we stand like rocks,
Through thick and thin, laughter unlocks.

A jellyfish smiles at our goofy dance,
We spin and twirl, oh what a chance!
Together we shout, as crabs start to flee,
Our friendship flows wild, like wavy sea.

So when the tide pulls, we hold on tight,
In every splash, we find our delight.
Through waves of life, we'll always float,
In this crazy ocean, that's our boat!

Shimmering Bonds

In the disco light, we twirl and sway,
Our shimmering bonds brighten the day.
With mismatched socks and funky shoes,
We can't help but dance, it's what we choose.

The DJ spins, our feet take flight,
We laugh at each other, it feels so right.
Each twirl and turn, a promise made,
In this kaleidoscope, no moment's delayed.

As we prance around like festive bears,
The world fades away, who even cares?
Our glowing spirits together unite,
Like silly stars twinkling in the night.

So here's to the magic that makes us whole,
With every heartbeat, we reel and roll.
These bonds we share, forever spun,
In this dance of life, we have our fun!

The Dance of Giving

Under the moon, we spin with delight,
In the dance of giving, we shine so bright.
With giggles and gifts exchanged with flair,
We toss our worries into the air.

Each gift a jest, wrapped in a pun,
A rubber chicken, oh what fun!
We trade our quirks, both big and small,
In this funny show, we have a ball.

With a wink and a nod, friendship's the key,
We make it work, just you and me.
Through laughter and joy, the night unfolds,
These gifts of laughter are pure gold.

So let's keep dancing under the stars,
Spreading our giggles, no need for cars.
In this fun fiesta of giggly cheer,
Together we dance, year after year!

Flickers of Connection

In the market, a spark caught my eye,
A cat in a bowtie, oh me, oh my!
He strutted with style, a real fancy chap,
While I nearly stumbled in my own mishap.

Juggling two donuts, one wobbly spree,
I tossed them up high, oh, where could they be?
Right into the hands of a clown with a grin,
And laughter erupted, oh where to begin?

Friends from afar, we danced in the park,
Tripped over our feet, but ignited a spark.
With bubbles and giggles, we twirled 'round and back,
Creating a canvas of joy that's uncracked.

So here's to the days filled with wild, silly cheer,
Where connection's a dance that brings everyone near.
Through laughter and mishaps, let joy freely flow,
In the ring of our smiles, together we glow.

Serpentine Threads of Fate

Tangled in yarn, we sat for a while,
Knitting our dreams, oh what a strange style!
With stitches and snickers, we crafted a tale,
That tangled us more, oh goodness, we'd fail!

A squirrel joined in, brave and quite bold,
He swiped our snacks, oh what a sight to behold!
Chasing him round, our laughter took flight,
In the chase for the nuts, we forgot the long night.

We crafted a necklace from popsicle sticks,
The masterpiece shone, it was quite a mix!
Onlookers chuckled, as we wore our grand best,
There's magic in chaos, we're truly blessed!

So here's to the moments all tangled and bright,
Where threads weave together, all wrong feels all right.
With each absurd twist, a smile does thrive,
In the loop of our lives, we're happy and alive!

Heartfelt Reflections

In a park, a mirror stood tall and quite grand,
Reflecting our faces, both silly and planned.
With silly grimaces, we posed one by one,
Sharing our laughter, just having such fun.

A dog in a tutu came prancing on by,
He stole the show under the bright, sunny sky.
Chasing his tail, oh what a grand sight,
We rolled on the grass, laughter brought pure delight.

Cupcakes in hand, we made quite the mess,
With icing on noses, we must confess.
Toasting with sprinkles, we danced through the day,
Creating sweet memories in our own special way.

So here's to reflections, both honest and bright,
In the mirror of moments, we find pure delight.
With joy in our hearts, and smiles so wide,
The beauty of friendship, we cannot hide.

Symphonies of Togetherness

In a band of friends, we played with our hearts,
Banging on drums like a wild work of arts.
The spoons got involved, and oh what a scene,
With laughter and rhythm, we lost track of keen!

A flute joined the mix, off-key but with flair,
We crooned through the chaos, the joy in the air.
With twirls and with spins, doing silly old dances,
Taking grand bows, perfecting our chances.

Uneasy on toes, we tripped through the night,
With antics and giggles, it felt so just right.
Through harmonies messy, we found our own tune,
Creating a festival under the moon.

So here's to the symphonies made with a laugh,
Where each silly note became part of the path.
In the concert of friendship, our hearts find their way,
Together in laughter, we'll forever stay.

www.ingramcontent.com/pod-product-compliance
Lightning Source LLC
Chambersburg PA
CBHW070004300426
43661CB00141B/215